Multisensory Spelling

Teachers' Book
and
Kinaesthetic Activities
5

Months, days, colours and numbers

Sue Graves

Contents

Teachers' Notes

Kinaesthetic activities (p3-6)

It is suggested that, in the main, these activities should be teacher or adult helper led. However, a responsible child may be chosen to lead the activities at the teacher's discretion.

A list of the resources needed for each of these activities can be found at the top of each activity page.

Most activities can be scored to find a winner for each game. The scoring mechanism is described in each activity. However, this is not a prerequisite and the activities can all be played on a non-competitive basis, if wished.

Letter cards (p7-9)

The teacher could print these letters on to card or photocopy them on to card and laminate them if wished. It is suggested the cards could be used in group or pairs work or on an individual basis to secure spelling patterns for spelling days, months, colour and number words.

Hollow words (p10-15)

Use the hollow words to practise and reinforce spelling patterns of days, months, colour and number words.
There are several ways of using these words.
Invite the children to reinforce the spelling of colour words by colouring them in appropriately eg colour the word 'pink' pink.
Ask the children to colour words containing the same letter sequences in the same colour, eg months ending in 'ember' colour this sequence green.
Cut out the words and paste them on to card to make word cards for spelling and reading practice.
Children might like to use the word wall as a record of spelling achievement, colouring in each word learned.

Word list (p16)

The words are listed alphabetically, rather than in order of appearance. It is suggested that where further practice of months, numbers or days is required, the teacher encourages the children to practise the words in their correct order to help the children recall the sequences.

Pupil record charts (p17-20)

There are four sections to the pupil record chart; one section per learning style. It is suggested that the teacher records details of the pupil's achievement in each activity. At the end of each section there is a learning style rating. Use this to establish the child's preferred learning style, circle the number that most closely indicates the child's preference for this learning style; 1 being the least preferred and 5 the most preferred.

Activities on CD

The interactive activities provide opportunities to practise days, months, colour and number words using visual, tactile and auditory learning styles. See page 2 for an overview of the activities on the CD.

Overview of CD-activities

Note: The icon in the top right hand corner of each activity indicates the main learning style addressed.

Activity	Main Learning Style
1	**Tactile**: Looking at numbers, finding and typing the number words.
2	**Auditory**: Listening to colour words; typing colour words.
3	**Visual**: Drag and drop exercise placing missing months into the right place on the calendar.
4	**Tactile**: Typing missing letters to spell the days of the week. Typing whole words.
5	**Auditory**: Identifying words and placing them into the correct category.
6	**Visual**: Identifying correct word from a choice of four words.
7	**Tactile**: Drag and drop exercise to complete the spellings of the months of the year and typing whole words.
8	**Auditory**: Finding answers to clues. Drag and drop exercise.
9	**Visual**: Matching word sums to make pairs. Drag and drop exercise.
10	**Tactile**: Unscrambling letters to type the correct spellings for days of the week.
11	**Auditory**: Listening to spellings to identify colour words.
12	**Visual**: Sentence completion work, using drag and drop.
13	**Tactile**: Making sets of words and then typing them.
14	**Auditory**: Identifying and typing words in sets according to their end sounds.
15	**Visual**: Identifying correct word from lists of words.
16	**Tactile**: Deleting incorrect words from pairs of words. Typing correct words.
17	**Auditory**: Identifying matching pairs of letters in words and typing them.
18	**Visual**: Identifying word shapes. Drag and drop exercise.
19	**Tactile**: Typing sets of 4 new sentences by changing one word at a time.
20	**Auditory**: Identifying same and different pairs of words.
21	**Visual**: Finding and matching same words in strings of mixed words.
22	**Tactile**: Identifying and deleting incorrect sentences in pairs of sentences. Typing correct sentences.
23	**Auditory**: Using clues given to identify days, months, number and colour words. Drag and drop exercises. Typing whole words.
24	**Visual**: Word search activity finding words with 'een' endings. Typing words.

Kinaesthetic activity 1
Spin, walk and spell

Group work

What you need:

Copies of the letter cards a-z.
Simple spinner.

What you do:

1. Place the letter cards in a large circle in the middle of the floor or playground.
2. Place the spinner in the middle of the circle.
3. Choose a child to spin the spinner.
4. Ask the child to suggest a day, month, colour or number word beginning with the letter at which the spinner stops.
5. Ask him or her to choose a child to spell the word.
6. The child must spell the word by walking round the circle and standing by the correct letters in the correct sequence, reading out the letters they choose.
7. If correct, the child spins the spinner and chooses another child to spell a day, month, colour or number word.
8. Award a point for each correct spelling.
9. The winner is the child with the most points.
   (Note: Where the spinner stops on a tricky letter such as 'q' or 'x' allow the child to have another turn with the spinner.)

Kinaesthetic activity 2
Sequence and spell

Group work:
For days of the week you need 8 children.
For months of the year you need 13 children.

What you need:

A set of hollow word cards for either the days of the week or the months of the year.

What you do:

1.   Choose one child (Child A) to have the first turn.
2.   Ask the other children to each take a word card and to hold it up in front of them.
3.   Ask Child A to place the children in the right order to show either the months of the year or the days of the week in the correct sequence.
4.   When the correct sequence has been achieved, ask the children to turn their cards over so that the words cannot be seen.
5.   Now ask Child A to stand by each child in turn and spell aloud the word on their card.
6.   Children holding the cards should check that spellings are correct. Award one point for each correct spelling.
7.   When Child A has spelled all the words, choose another child to take a turn.
8.   To make a simpler game after section 3, Child A could point to a child and ask him or her to say the word they are holding (1 point) and then spell it (5 points).

Kinaesthetic activity 3
Colour, spin and spell

Group activity

What you need:

A circular piece of card marked with segments each of
a different colour. A thin piece of wood is pushed through
the centre of the card to make a basic spinner.

What you do:

1. Explain to the children that they are going to spell colour words.
2. Ask them to take turns to spin the spinner.
3. The child spells the colour indicated when the spinner comes to rest.
4. Award a point for each correct spelling.
5. The winner is the child with the most points at the end of the session.
6. Alternatively, a point could be awarded for each letter in a word spelled correctly, eg red = 3 points, blue = 4 points.

Kinaesthetic activity 4
The numbers game

Group work

What you need:

Letter cards. (you may need more than one set)
Selection of number cards, as required.

What you do:

1. Place the letter cards face up at one end of the school hall.
2. Choose children to hold up number cards as required.
3. Choose a child (Child A) to have the first turn.
4. Ask Child A to look at each number card and run and get the correct letter cards to spell the number words. The child should place the letter cards in the correct sequence at the feet of the child holding the matching number card.
5. Award a point for each correct spelling.
6. When the number cards have been spelled, replace the letter cards and choose another child to take a turn.
7. The winner is the child with the most points at the end of the session.
8. Alternatively, teams of 3 could choose to spell 3 different number words in a given time. Points are awarded for the number of letters in the word, eg seven = 5 points.

Letter cards a-h

Print or paste onto card prior to doing the activities.

a	b	c
d	e	f
g	h	

Letter cards i-q

Print or paste onto card prior to doing the activities.

i j k

l m n

o p q

Letter cards r-z

Print or paste onto card prior to doing the activities.

r　　s　　t

u　　v　　w

x　　y　　z

Hollow words

January	February	March
April	May	June
July	August	September
October	November	December

January	February	March
April	May	June
July	August	September
October	November	December

Hollow words

Monday	Tuesday	Wednesday
Thursday	Friday	Saturday
Sunday	day	week
	month	

Monday	Tuesday	Wednesday
Thursday	Friday	Saturday
Sunday	day	week
	month	

Hollow words

black	blue	brown
green	grey	orange
pink	purple	red
white	yellow	colour

black	blue	brown
green	grey	orange
pink	purple	red
white	yellow	colour

Hollow words

one	two	three
four	five	six
seven	eight	nine
	ten	

one	two	three
four	five	six
seven	eight	nine
	ten	

Hollow words

eleven	twelve	thirteen
fourteen	fifteen	sixteen
seventeen	eighteen	nineteen
	twenty	

eleven	twelve	thirteen
fourteen	fifteen	sixteen
seventeen	eighteen	nineteen
	twenty	

Hollow words

thirty	forty	fifty
sixty	seventy	eighty
ninety	hundred	number

thirty	forty	fifty
sixty	seventy	eighty
ninety	hundred	number

Word list

A April
August

B black
blue
brown

C colour

D day
December

E eight
eighteen
eighty
eleven

F February
fifteen
fifty
five
forty
four
fourteen
Friday

G green
grey

H hundred

J January
July
June

M March
May
Monday
month

N nine
nineteen
ninety
November
number

O October
one
orange

P pink
purple

R red

S Saturday
September
seven
seventeen
seventy
six
sixteen
sixty
Sunday

T ten
thirteen
thirty
three
Thursday
Tuesday
twelve
twenty
two

W Wednesday
week
white

Y yellow

Pupil record sheet

Name: _____

Class/ Year group: _____

Learning style: TACTILE

Activity	Date	Comments
1		
4		
7		
10		
13		
16		
19		
22		

Learning style rating: 1   2   3   4   5

(circle rating which most indicates preference)

Pupil record sheet

Name: _____

Class/ Year group: _____

Learning style: AUDITORY

Activity	Date	Comments
2		
5		
8		
11		
14		
17		
20		
23		

Learning style rating: 1   2   3   4   5

(circle rating which most indicates preference)

Pupil record sheet

Name: _____

Class/ Year group: _____

Learning style: VISUAL

Activity	Date	Comments
3		
6		
9		
12		
15		
18		
21		
24		

Learning style rating: 1   2   3   4   5

(circle rating which most indicates preference)

Pupil record sheet

Name: _____

Class/ Year group: _____

Learning style: KINAESTHETIC

Activity	Date	Comments
K1		
K2		
K3		
K4		

Learning style rating: 1   2   3   4   5

(circle rating which most indicates preference)